1

THE FINANCIAL MIRACLE PRAYER

THE PRAYER THAT BRINGS FINANCIAL

MIRACLES QUICKLY

2

FRANCIS K.D. JONAH

3

TABLE OF CONTENTS

IMPORTANT

My name is Francis Jonah. I believe all things are possible. It is because of this belief that I have achieved so much in life. This belief extends to all. I believe every human being is equipped to succeed in every circumstance, regardless of the circumstance.

I know the only gap that exists between you and what you need to achieve or overcome is knowledge.

People are destroyed for lack of knowledge.

It is for this reason that I write short practical books that are so simple, people begin to experience immediate results as evidenced by the many testimonies I receive on daily basis for my various books.

This book is no exception. You will obtain results because of it.

Send me an email for a FREE copy of my book

"All Things Are Possible"

My email is **drfrancisjonah@gmail.com**

INTRODUCTION

We have all wanted financial miracles before. Some of us have actually had financial miracles before.

The question you should ask yourself is, is a miracle God's best for you?

In this book you will learn how to receive financial miracles. You will also learn how to specifically deal with hindrances to financial miracles.

Finally, you will learn how to walk in something better than miracles in your finances.

CHAPTER ONE:

THE FINANCIAL MIRACLE PRAYER

Have you ever been in a financial fix before?

A fix so bad you needed to be dug out of it?

Well, most of us have and we are free today enjoying peace and financial prosperity.

The prayer I will introduce here is a simple prayer.

To understand more on prayer, read my book on 100% Answered prayer.

It will revolutionise your prayer life.

When you are in need of a financial miracle, you can pray for one. But the prayer I will introduce is not the kind we all are used to praying and receiving no results.

It is an easier way to pray and more effective.

After that prayer, you need to deal with hindrances and oppositions to that prayer.

This is because God uses men to bless us financially. If they are hindered, our answers also delay.

The prayer:

Father, In The name of Jesus, I thank you that you always supply my need.

9

I acknowledge the fact that you love me and will never leave me nor forsake me.

Thank you for your grace and provision in my life.

Thank you for your son Jesus whom you gave freely.

Thank you that with Jesus you have also supplied this.........amount .... that I need.

I bless you father and thank you because I have received it.

I celebrate you because it is mine now.

All glory, honour and adoration to your holy name.

Thank you that you have done it for me. Amen

After praying the prayer of thanksgiving for the financial miracle, you need to now intercede for whoever God is using to bring the need to you. At this point you must recognize that God has already done his part.

The prayer:

Father, In the name of Jesus, I thank you for whoever you are supplying my financial needs through.

I thank you for their lives, their business, their job and their families.

I pray and command every hindrance that will prevent them from bringing the supply to give way right now. IN Jesus name.

I pray and deal with any doubt or affliction that will prevent them from heeding to your call to supply.

Devil and all your cohorts, take your hands of these people, take your hands of their finances, take your hands of their health, take your hands of their thoughts, and all that belongs to them in the name of Jesus.

Devil and all your cohorts, take your hands of my finances too. In JESUS NAME.

After rebuking the devil as God has commanded you to, you go back to thanking God.

The prayer:

Father, in the name of Jesus, I thank you and honour you.

I bless your holy name and I magnify you.

You deserve all the glory and all the praise.

I love and I worship you.

I thank you for the authority and power that you have given me.

13

Thank you for unlimited grace that is at work in my life.

Thank you for the finances you have sent my way.

Keep Thanking God and speak in tongues if you can. Your financial miracle is already released.

CHAPTER TWO:

MIRACLES ARE NOT GOD'S BEST

Anywhere you see financial miracles abound, it is a clear indication of a lot of financial crisis.

It simply means people are not walking in the blessings of God which is already given to them according to Ephesians 1:3.

It means people are not using the power of wealth that God has deposited within them.

There may be exceptional cases but the ideal plan of God is for us to have more than enough to meet the needs of others.

That way you will be walking in the blessing of God.

You will be walking in financial prosperity instead of always waiting for a miracle.

- Your hands are blessed; you have the power to make wealth. Set new financial goals and work at them as a response of the power of God within you.

Work at them as a response to the blessing of God over your life.

Do not give up at the first opposition or negative sign. Know that you are blessed, you do not fail and you have wealth making power within you.

Figure out where the problem is and work at it till you succeed financially.

You, my dear are blessed and have all it takes to make it financially.

CHAPTER THREE:

TESTIMONIES

HOW I RECEIVED MONEY FOR MY CAR

I had prayed and also received the answer to my prayer for a car.

Most of us do not know how to receive answers to prayer. (Read 100% Answered Prayer for that teaching).

After a year, I had still not received it. One day, I got tired and dealt with the hindrances to that prayer and sowed a seed of fuel into someone's car.

A week later, I received money to buy a car.

The person told me later that God had spoken to him a year earlier to give me money for a car but he couldn't do it because his business began to struggle.

This time round, he said he had received a big contract and thus had the means to obey what God had told him to do.

I took me a year or more to receive the car physically.

Not because God did not answer but because the person to bring it was hindered in his business.

HOW I GAVE SOMEONE MONEY FOR TWO YEARS HOUSE RENT AFTER GOD HAD SPOKEN TO ME THREE YEARS EARLIER.

God spoke to me to get money for two years house rent for someone.

I told him to come for money when he was ready for the house. The year God spoke to me and I told him to come, he never came.

The next year that he came, I didn't get the money I was expecting to give him. It was because the one to give me the money I had worked for just refused to give me although he had given all others who worked. (It was a hindrance)

The third year, to my amazement, this man gave me twice the amount.

I quickly called the person and gave to him his due for the rent.

He said, he thanked God for finances that week after he checked his account and found nothing in it and dealt with every hindrance to his finances.

Later that week I gave him the money.

He got the money in the third year not because that is when God asked me to give it to him but hindrances kept the money from getting to him for those three years.

God had answered him three years ago.

It is the same with you. Your financial miracle is already released. Deal with the hindrances and keep thanking God.

Other books by FRANCIS JONAH you must read:

Healing the sick in 5 minutes

Powerful Prayer Method for All prayers

Achieve something now

Be Happy Now: No more depression

The healing Miracle prayer

PRAYER OF SALVATION:

The greatest miracle is not that eyes have been opened, the deaf heard, Jesus Christ walked on water, or you bought a house, etc.

The greatest miracle is SALVATION.

The greatest miracle happens when you give your life to Jesus. The bible said in 2corinthians 5:17;

"Therefore if any man be in Christ, he is a new creature: old things are passed away; behold, all things are become new"

The moment you give your life to Jesus Christ, every negative thing in your life comes to an end.

24

If you have not met Jesus, I want to pray specially for you.

Just pray this prayer after me;

"Lord Jesus Christ, I come to you today as a sinner, I cannot help myself. Please forgive me for all my sins, I believe in my heart that you died for me and you were raised up by God.

Today, I accept you lord as Jesus Christ as my lord and savior.

Cleanse me with your precious blood; deliver me from sin to serve you. Thank you, Jesus, for saving me. Now I know that I am born again by your mighty name... Amen Send me an email for a FREE copy of my book

"All Things Are Possible"

My email is **drfrancisjonah@gmail.com**

26

Made in the USA
Las Vegas, NV
01 April 2025

20379550R00016